Venture into the Everglades

Niurka Castaneda
Masha Andreoni, LCSW

For information about special discounts for bulk purchases, please contact AMOR umbrella at bulk@amorumbrella.com

Softcover ISBN: 978-1-7364815-0-9

Ebook ISBN: 978-1-7364815-1-6

Hardcover ISBN: 979-8-9855579-5-4

Library of Congress Control Number: 2022903017

This is a work of creative nonfiction. Some parts have been fictionalized in various degrees, for various purposes.

Cover Design by: Alejandro Castaneda

Interior: Niurka Castaneda

Photo on page 9, 58 ©Evangelina Andreoni, 8 ©Neal Stark, 59 ©Christine M. Sanchez, 35, The U.S. National Archives - 36, 45 public domain, 10 - 31, 38 - 44, 48 - 53 ©Niurka Castaneda

Printed by Ventures C & A LLC in the United States of America

1st Edition 15 Feb 2022

Ventures C & A LLC

Miami, FL 33197

www.amorumbrella.com

Dedication & Acknowledgement

For our families,
And for each and every person who has helped us believe in ourselves, in a mission greater than ourselves and in the great potential each of us has to heal through the power of love, hope and storytelling.

Venture into the Everglades
Table of Content

PROLOGUE

A short story that introduces you to the majestic Everglades, also known as the **"River of Grass."**

EVERGLADES

"There are no other Everglades in the world. They are, they have always been, one of the unique regions of the earth, remote, never wholly known. Nothing anywhere else is like them"

Marjory Stoneman Douglas

Have you ever visited the Everglades?

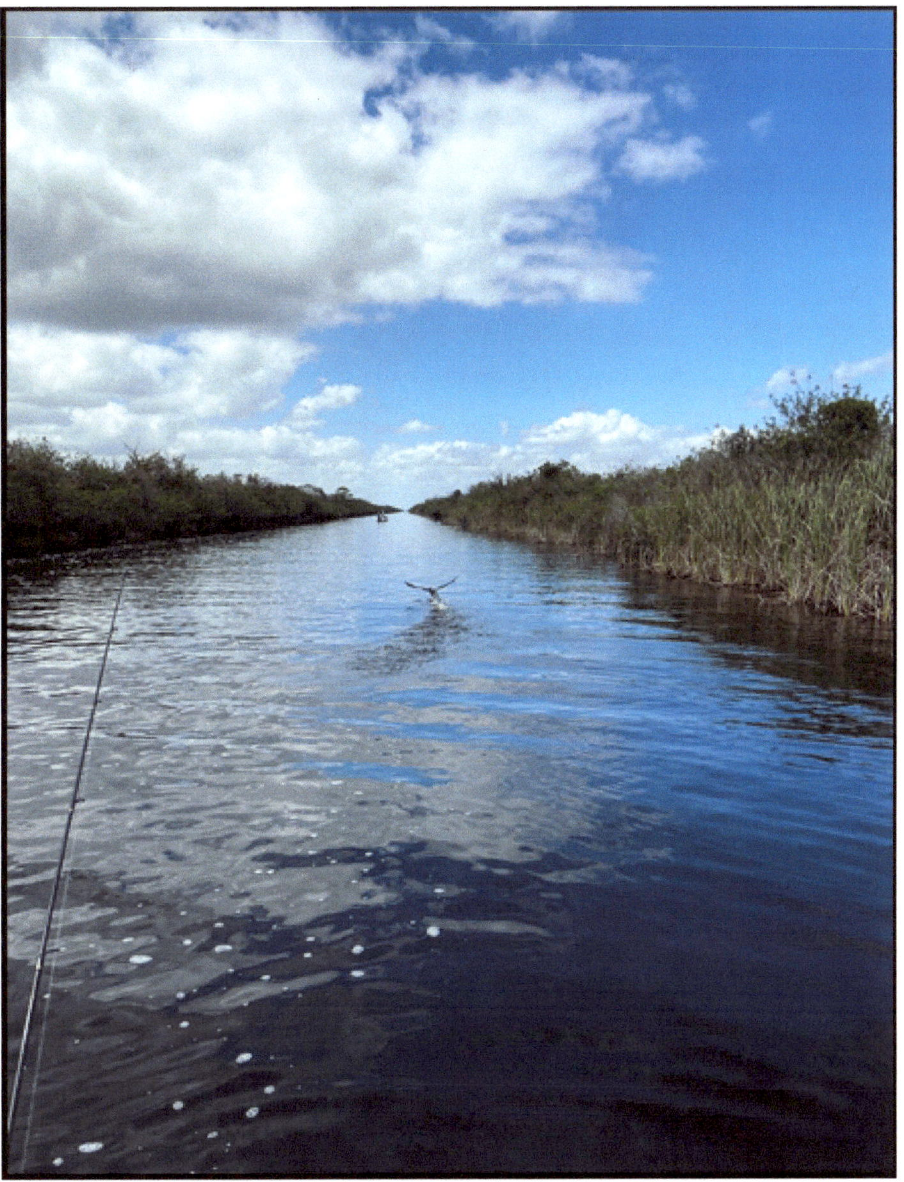

National Everglades Park / Photo: Niurka Castaneda

We did!

It was Joe, her kids, Lulu, Masha, Captain and me…

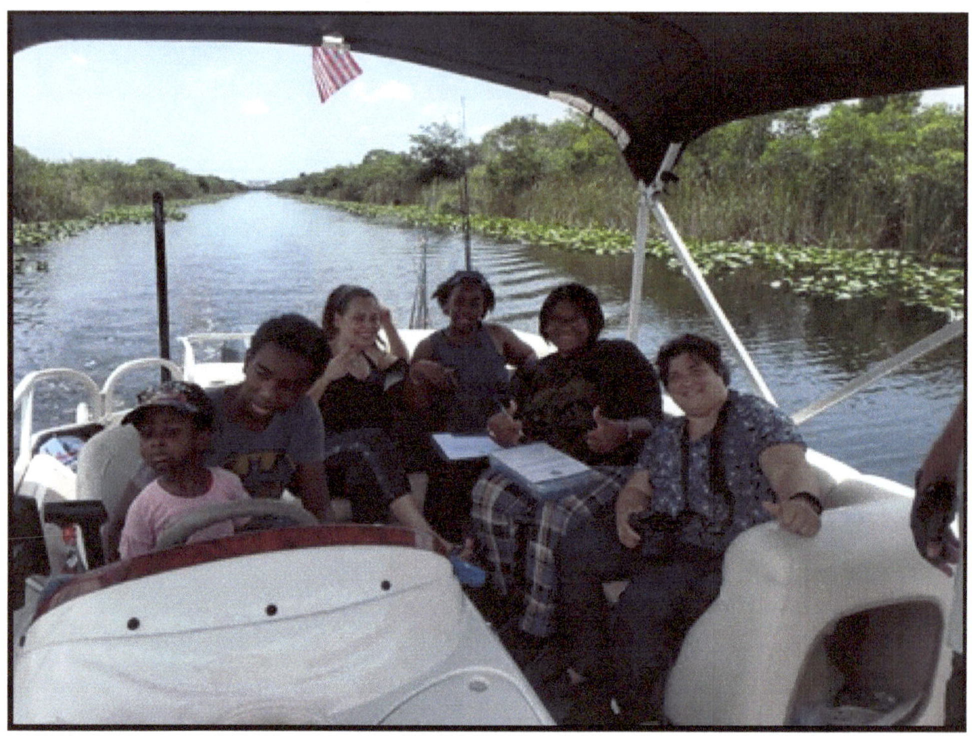

Photo: CPT Neal Stark

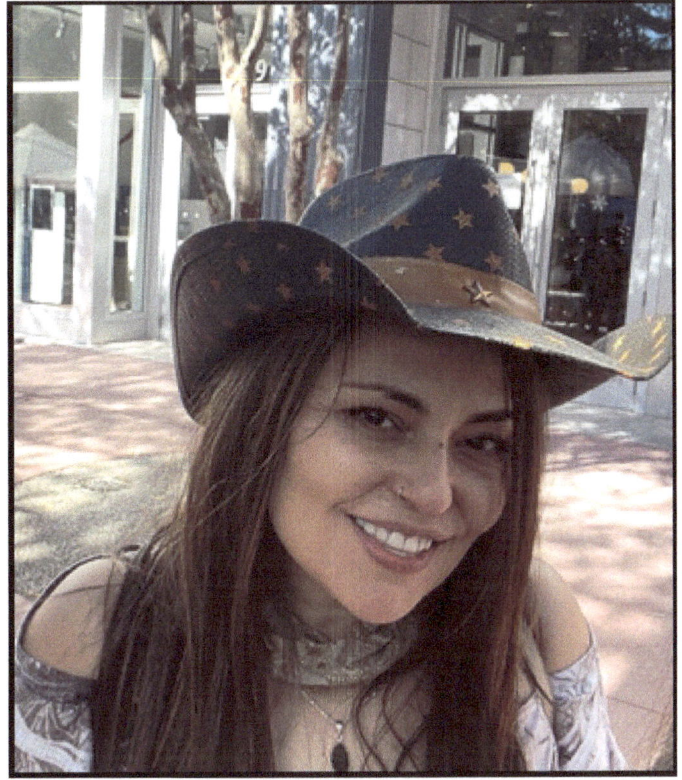

Photo: Evangelina Andreoni

Masha was the one that suggested and organized this trip. She is also helping me with this publication. As a licensed clinical social worker who is passionate about, dedicated to, and grateful for Veterans, she has chosen to dedicate her time/practice to serving those who have served and their families. Because of her strong belief in the therapeutic value of combining recreational therapy with traditional therapy…she coordinated this trip with her friend, Captain Neal Stark (Cpt.)

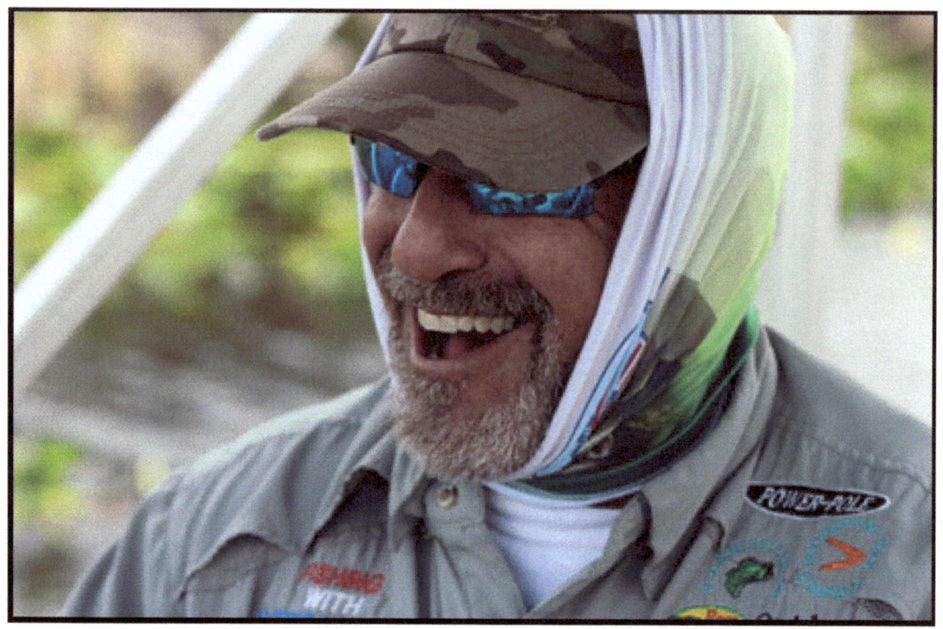

Photos: Niurka Castaneda

Captain Neal is the founder of Fishing with America's Finest (FWAF). This is a charitable nonprofit organization that is dedicated to providing therapeutic piscatorial (fishing) outings to Veterans and their families for the past twelve years. He is a professional tournament angler and has a deep love for the Everglades and extensive knowledge of the land and its ecosystem..

Hi

I'm Niurka and I am a female Veteran.

I am very well aware of the challenges and obstacles I have had to face before, during, and after my time in active duty.

I am grateful that on this day I had an open mind and an open heart to do something very different.

A fun outing during this period in my life was a completely foreign concept. I took a chance.

I can honestly say that I am grateful because I went against what felt "comfortable" yesterday, and today, the explorer in me has come back to life.

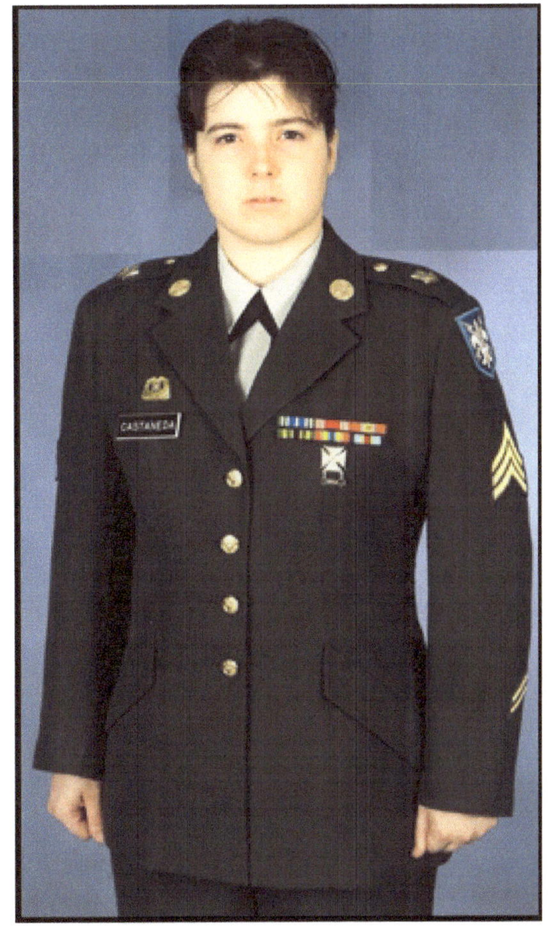

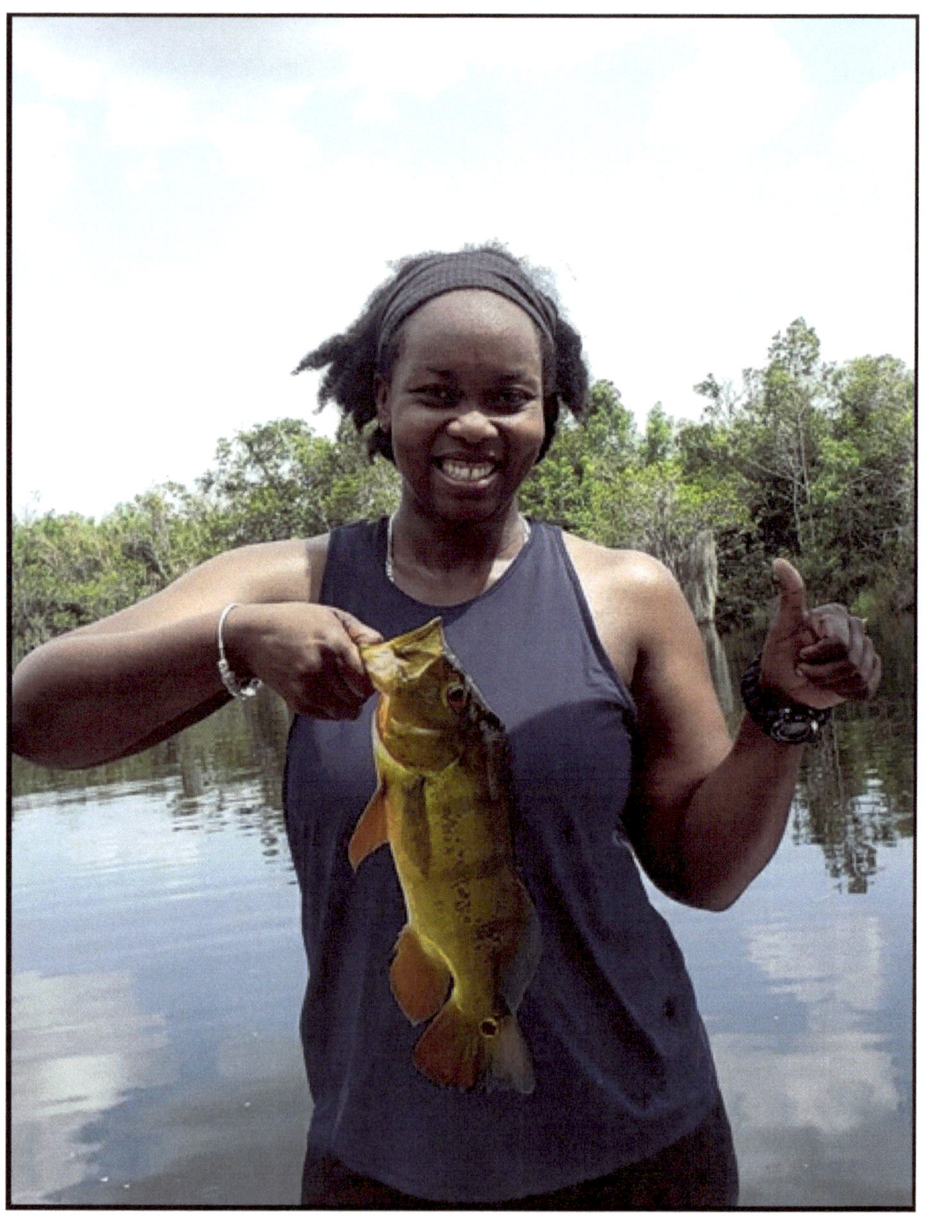

Thumbs up /Photo: Niurka Castaneda

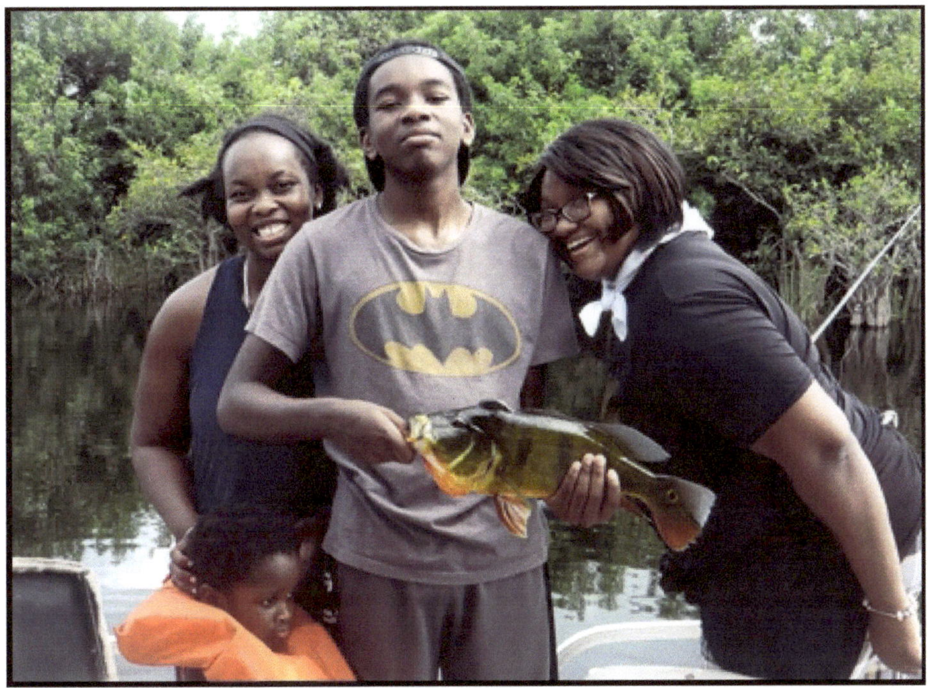

The Catch /Photo: Niurka Castaneda

Joe and Lulu are also female Veterans who own their own life stories and have overcome some challenges too.

Together, we embarked on an unforgettable journey to explore the swamplands and to learn about the rich ecosystem hiding in our very own backyard. It was truly a welcomed adventure.

Personally, this adventure left a profound impression and touched my HEART.

Why? Because it was HEALING… It was PEACEFUL… it was MAGICAL.

We escaped the noise of the city and enjoyed the tranquility of the slow-flowing water. Being able to take our minds off of everything that usually weighs us down was BEYOND relaxing. It was definitely the perfect place to rest and become one with nature. We were actually able to bask in the quietness of it all.

It was BEYOND just an adventure. More than a fishing trip, it was a transformational experience…

The Everglades National Park is located just forty miles west of Miami, our current hometown. There is no shortage of exciting and wonderful activities for the whole family to experience.

Brave adventurous souls can be seen hiking, canoeing, kayaking, boating, biking, and camping in this ultimate wilderness wonderland.

A fishing trip is an activity that most (especially Veterans) could benefit from, even if one has never fished before. It is both peaceful and helpful.

Between the participants, the guide, and mother nature we definitely formed a stronger bond on this day.

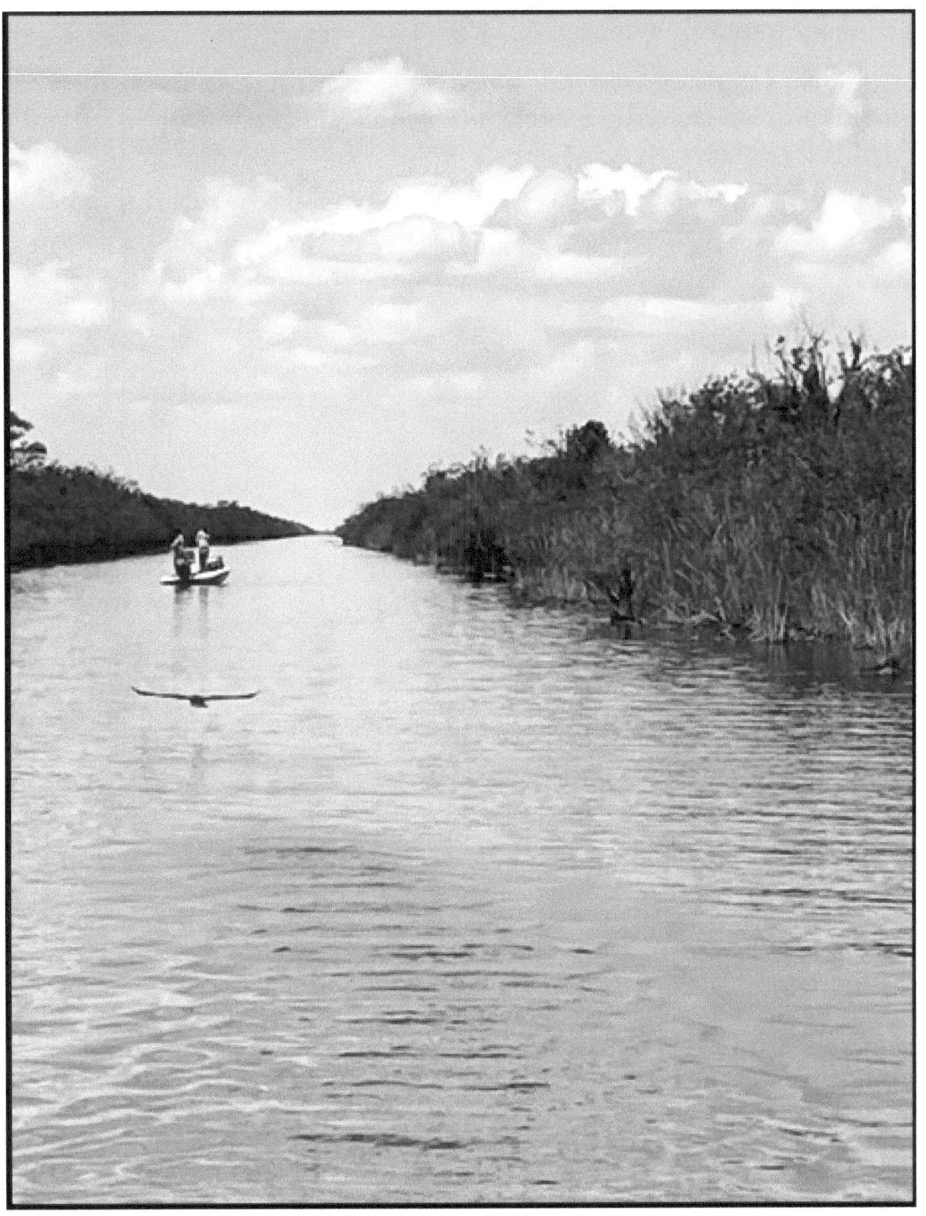

We Dare/ Photo: Niurka Castaneda

These types of experiences create camaraderie and provide a safe space to share about whatever burdens one may be carrying.

Fishing has documented results as a valuable recreational therapeutic alternative. This activity encompasses mindfulness, meditation...simply being in the present moment.

You can escape the noise of the city and enjoy the tranquility of the slow flowing water which is very relaxing. It is the perfect place to rest while observing nature.

Between the beautiful setting and the great company...this trip truly had a calming effect on us all.

Amidst the tranquil waters we ventured off on Captain's pontoon boat. It was nearly impossible for us not to escape to our collective happy place. Besides just the moving waters, we were surrounded by a historic nature-filled wonderland. It is easy to see how we all found a sense of peace. Just by taking a chance and participating, we all experienced a much-needed break from our daily stressors. We were definitely brought to the present day's moment. We got to truly unplug for a change.

The sentiment was written all over our faces, our cheerful smiles, and our eyes as we posed for pictures. Our moods were greatly improved. We spent the day joking, talking, and sharing from the heart.

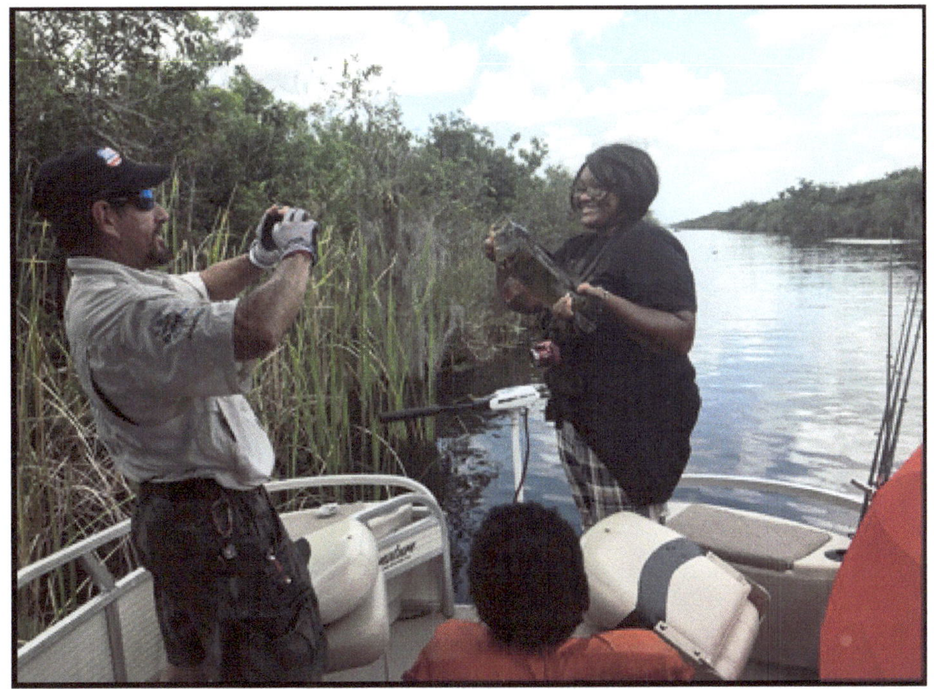

Smile / Photo: Niurka Castaneda

This was a stark contrast from our collective moods just before we got onto the water. The mood before our adventure was quiet and heavy, as we were mostly focused on what our yesterdays and tomorrows had to bring.

For Veterans and single mothers, our day-to-day activities/responsibilities tend to be very mission oriented and BUSY. Between family, educational goals, work, medical appointments (etc.)…We are ALWAYS on the go!!! Even though we may not have considered fishing as an enjoyable pastime prior to this day, we were able to experience the therapeutic value in disconnecting and relaxing for a change.

Towards the end of our little adventure some kept fishing and others simply sat back to enjoy the peaceful boat ride. Well, that is everyone except "Little Hillary." She spent most of her day entertaining the rest of us with her singing, dancing, and improvising...all while holding and twirling a red "Amor" umbrella.

This happy chirpy creative little human bird sang her HUGE heart out. It was definitely a charming moment that added much levity to an already incredible day. We were glad to have captured these precious moments in pictures and videos.

Some lines from Lil' Hillary's Song:

"It is a rainy day…
It is a sunny day…
It is a fun day…"

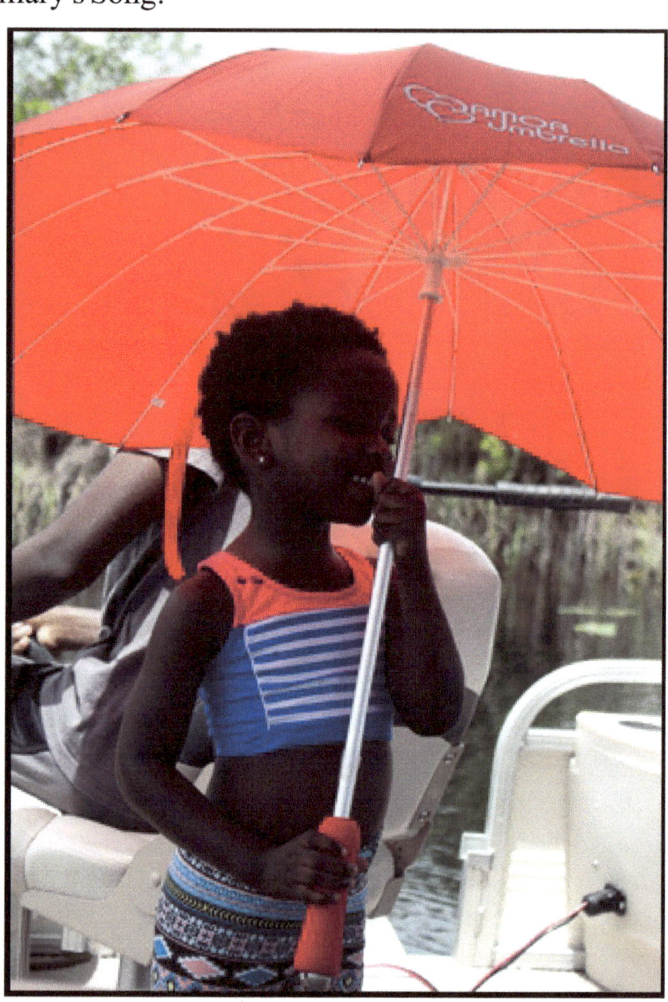

Lil' Hillary/ Photo: Niurka Castaneda

We all took turns trying to catch fish. Some were successful, others, not so much. :)

Fishing requires technique. Upon catching a fish, Captain Neal showed us how to carefully take out the hook in order not to hurt it. We then released them back into the waters as quickly and calmly as possible. The fish were unharmed.

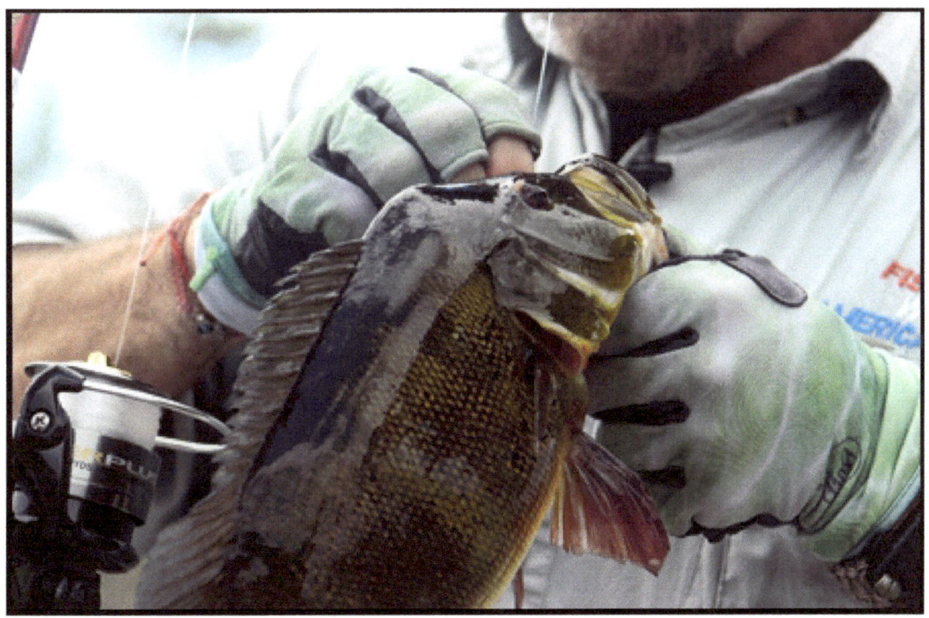

Off the Hook / Photo: Niurka Castaneda

This catch and release method Captain Neal practices allows for fish to remain plentiful and reproduce in the Everglades ecosystem. It also ensures that future generations can enjoy the same activities we did on this glorious day.

The Everglades came alive as Captain gifted us with stories. He talked about the flora and fauna that surrounded us. He told us about the "Freshwater Sloughs," a deep and marshy river dominated by the herbaceous specimens that function as the main routes of water flow.

He told us about the mangroves, adding that the red, black, and white fauna function as a nursery for many animals that call the Everglades their home.

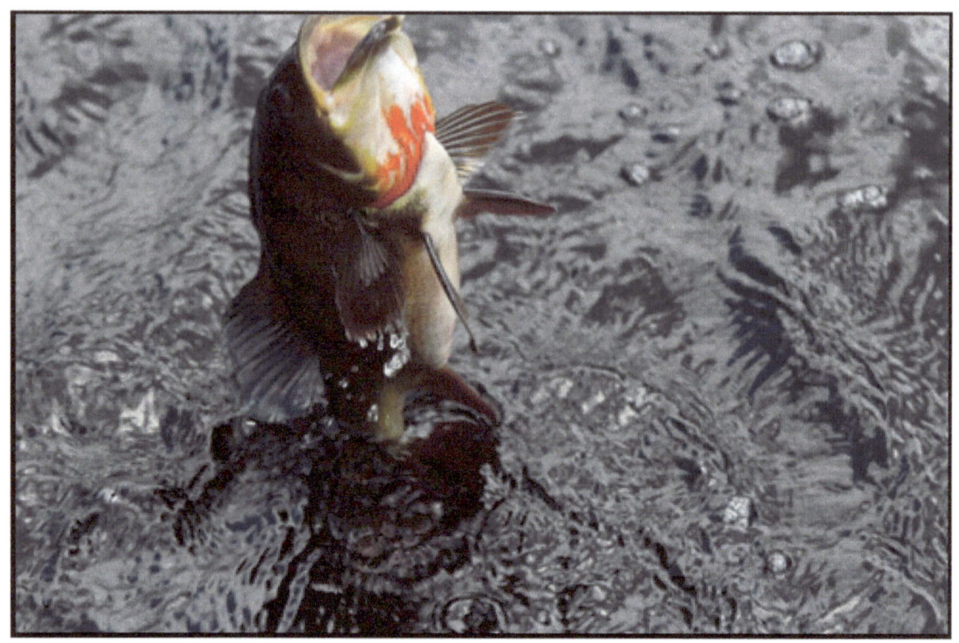

I Got Caught / Photo by Niurka Castaneda

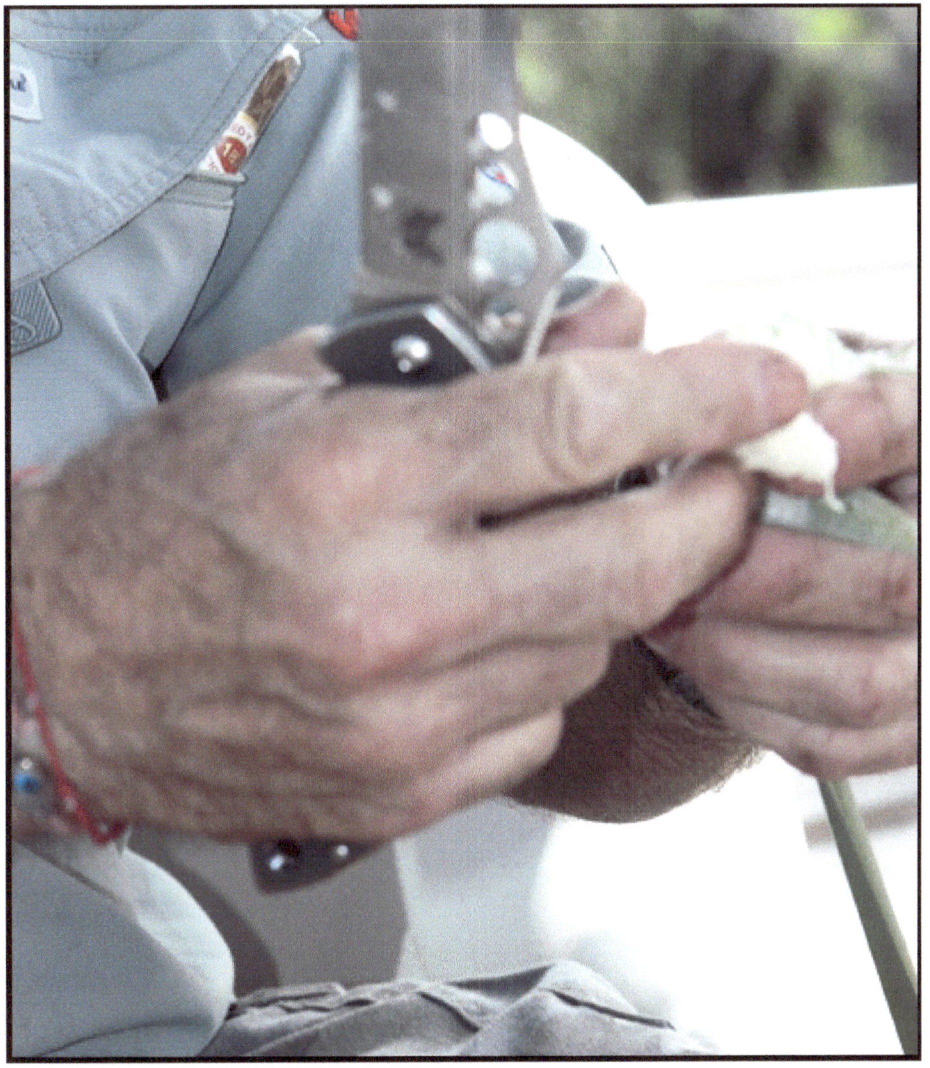

Mother Nature's gauze/ Photo: Niurka Castaneda

Mother Nature's gauze.

Captain Neal also demonstrated his survivalist skills by utilizing cattail frawns to make a makeshift bandage. These frawns are native to the Everglades and have come in handy for thousands of years. He showed us how to crush the leaves of a cattail frawn and make a poultice, which is a quick remedy for injuries when there isn't a first aid kit in sight.

He further explained that the sap from the Cattail frawn can also be applied to wounds and may even help with toothache pain. The Seminole and Miccosukee tribes of Indians utilized this often when in need, as their uses are vast and versatile. They can also be utilized as food, to make rope, mats, baskets, torches, and more.

Recreational Therapy Benefits

This particular trip really proved to us the POWERFUL benefits of recreational therapy. As mentioned before, Veterans experience many different types of challenges....especially after discharging from the military. Not to say one does not experience difficulties during their time in active duty, however upon discharge, the well-known structure, teamwork, and expectations are no longer well defined.

Upon discharge, many Veterans are left to navigate their "new normals" and often do so alone. Feelings of loss, anxiety, fear, hopelessness, depression, isolation etc. often accompany this transition. And while typically, friends and family may wish to alleviate the Veterans' stressors....relatability is often lacking.

Recreational therapy takes on many different forms and incorporates many different activities. Not to say conventional therapy with a licensed professional is not beneficial, but adding the recreational therapeutic modality helps put many discussed concepts to positive practical use. It is important to note that Recreational Therapy has been known and proven to help alleviate symptomatic feelings of depression and anxiety.

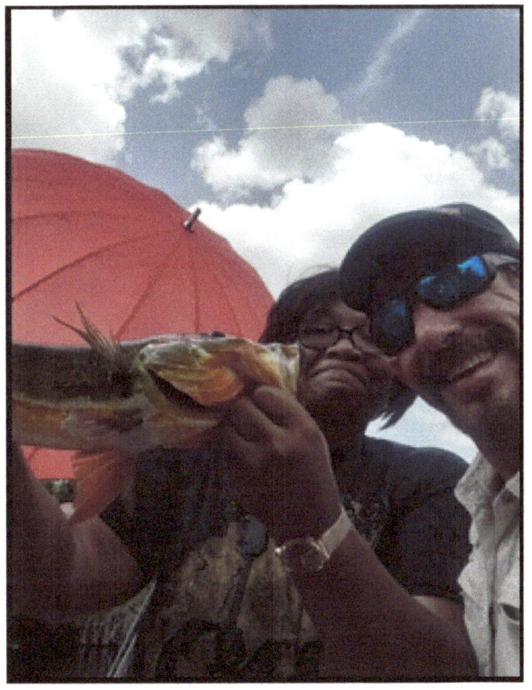

It isn't unusual for a Veteran to decline Recreational therapeutic activities at first due to hesitancy, but once dipping their toes in the proverbial waters (and NOT the swamp waters in the Everglades) it becomes a conducive component to conventional therapy. Not only does it bring about connection and camaraderie, but it often opens the doors to activities/talents one may never have known they encompass and enjoy.

This trip was not only centered on fishing for us. We incorporated photography, bird-watching, meditating, historical education, sharing and connecting. Most if not all would DEFINITELY do it again. As a matter of fact, this book is proof that the inspiration grows and has now been channeled into writing and reminiscing.

Do you know about the History of the Everglades National Park....?

Everglades originates from the word "forever" that means a "grassy open place." The Everglades was an ecosystem before it was declared a National Park.

Per the National Park Service (NPS):

> "The original Everglades used to reach all the way from the Orlando area to Florida Bay. It was a big wilderness of wetlands containing sawgrass marshes, freshwater sloughs, mangrove swamps, pine Rock-lands, and hardwood hammocks." (NPS)

Researchers have been able to trace human civilization to this area as far back as approximately 15,000 years ago.

The Everglades used to cover more than four thousand square miles. It runs from Lake Okeechobee to Florida's Southern tip. Today it is half the size it used to be one hundred years ago," according to Bergeron Everglades

Museum and Wildlife Foundation.

It was not until December 6th, 1947 that a small fraction of this vast ecosystem officially became known as the Everglades National Park.

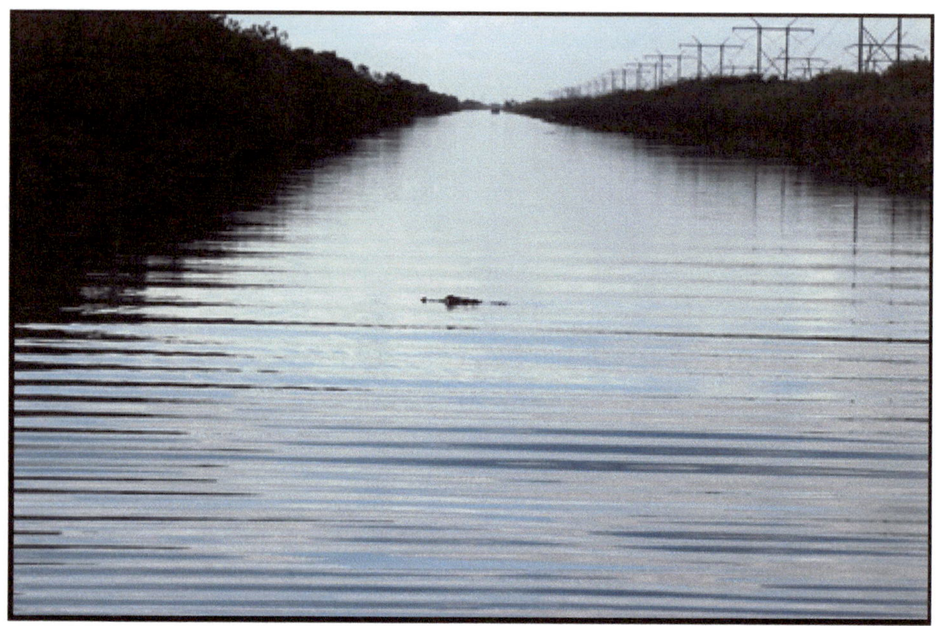

According to NPS:

> “This was the year the U.S. Senate declared 1.5M acres as part of a conservation area in order to protect this natural ecosystem.”(National Park Service)

Ernest F Coe's life driving purpose was to protect the Everglades. In order to accomplish this he founded the “Tropical Everglades National Park Association” in 1928. The name of the association later changed to "Everglades National Park Association.”

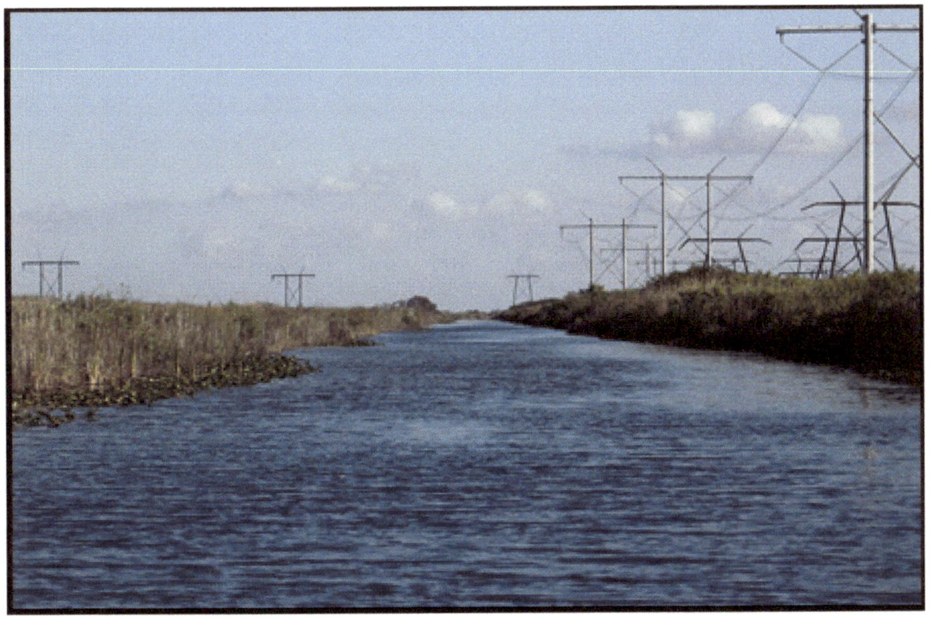

Save Me /Photo: Niurka Castaneda

All of the members of this association worked together in order to persuade Congress to appoint the Everglades as a national park. Nonetheless, due to the lack of funds needed to make this mission happen, it took another 14 years before this was considered a mission accomplished.

The "River of Grass" has an ecosystem unlike any other in the world. It is a slow-flowing river that is home to unique wildlife and a complex system of subtropical lakes, wetlands, and rivers, according to Live Science.

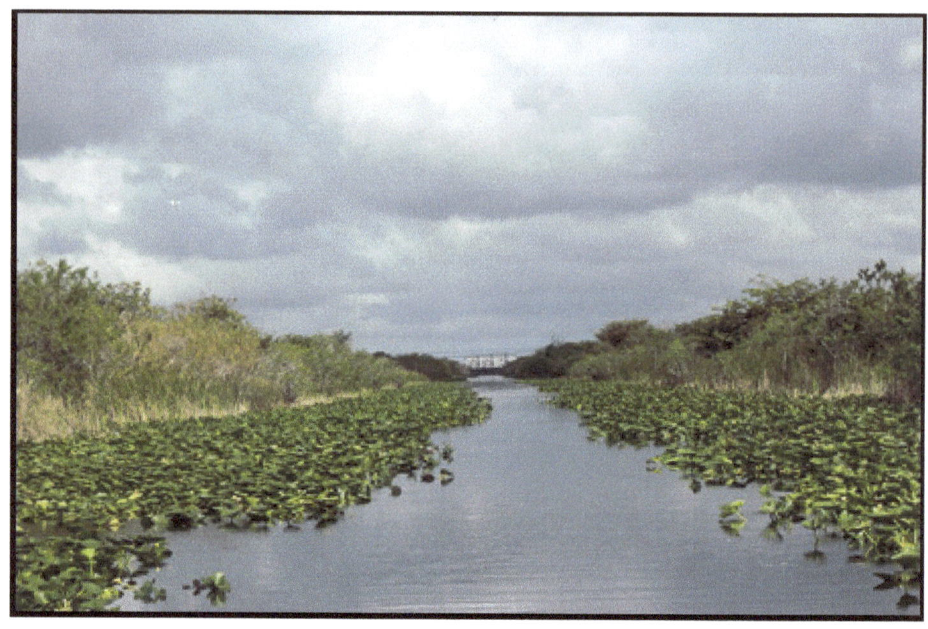

Help Me /Photo: Niurka Castaneda

It is not only the **United State's third biggest National Park** but a natural treasure that is sitting in our own backyard and has become a safe haven for many endangered species.

Prior to the Everglades becoming a National Park, the predominant public perception was that it was a "worthless swamp" and should be drained and developed. It was not only until Marjory Stoneman Douglas released her book "Everglades: River of Grass", that she was able to convince her book readers that this was a special magical place that needed their respect and protection. Marjory was a former Miami Herald newspaper's correspondent. She lived a full life until she passed away at 108 years old. Most of her life's work and passion were dedicated to restoring the Everglades.

Unfortunately due to mass development much of the Everglades has been chipped away.

> "The Everglades used to cover more than four thousand square miles. It runs from Lake Okeechobee to Florida's Southern tip. Today it is half

> the size it used to be one hundred years ago" according to Bergeron Everglades Museum and Wildlife Foundation.

This wild and exotic place, full of lush greenery and plentiful wildlife is unfortunately being chipped away by new development and draining of the wetlands. Due to these obstructions, the natural water flow has been altered.

According to Tommy Rodriguez from Visions of the Everglades:

> "History Ecology Preservation estimates it would take about thirty years and 7.8 billion dollars to accomplish the repair the systematic draining of the wetlands and altering of the water flow that was meant by mother nature to impede environmental disaster." (Tommy Rodriguez)

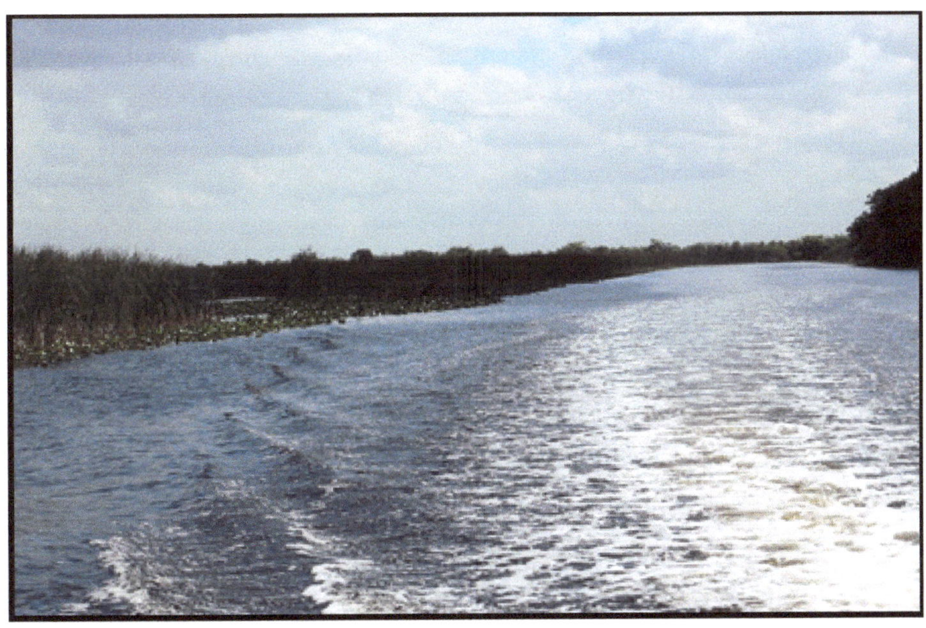

Everglades Flowing Waters /Photo: Niurka Castaneda

More Historical facts.... the Indigenous tribes native to the Everglades

After my visit to the Everglades I found out thru the Barrier Island Parks Society archives that there were natives living in the area since 15k+ years ago as a wooden carving of 12,000 years old found in Little Salt Spring indicated.

The original natives were the ancestors of the Calusa and the Tequesta natives Indians. The Mighty Calusa was a powerful tribe that occupied most of the territories from Lake Okeechobee to the Florida Keys.

As the dominant tribe, they received tribute from all other tribes and were responsible for killing Ponce de Leon in 1521

> "The last Calusa lived in the Keys. Around 270 Calusa were evacuated by Cubans and taken to Cuba in 1711, but over 200 died soon after the trip. Members of the aristocracy were among those who were evacuated "(Milanich 41)

When writing this book and doing more research, I actually found it fascinating to learn about the Calusa ties to my personal homeland, Cuba. In fact it is so fascinating to me, that I will be telling more of their story in another series later. Stay tuned.

Post the Calusa and Tequesta tribes came the Seminole and Miccosukee Indian tribes. Although originating in lands North of Florida, the Seminole Wars which spanned between 1817-1859 pushed the natives further south inhabiting the Everglades.

There are currently 6 Indian reservations (Seminole and Miccosukee) found in modern day Florida. These tribes are closely associated with the Everglades. Although too much of a rich and arduous history to include in this short publication, today's Seminole and Miccosukee Indian Reservations provide tourist attractions encompassing educational/historical tours, alligator wrestling, air boat rides and much much more.

But WAIT, there's more....

The Everglades also has somewhat of a sinister past too. Tales about The Lost City (also known as "The Ghost Village") a small site located about eight miles south of "Alligator Alley," have inspired thrilling stories full of gore and mysterious disappearances for centuries.

Remote and isolated, it was, and is, the perfect hideout for criminals and shifty characters to conceal their criminal endeavors. More than one body has been found belly up, floating on top of its waters.

WHO DID IT?

Hard to tell…

Edgar J Watson was a sugarcane plantation owner who died a notorious serial killer in the Everglades.

John Ashley was known as the "King of the Everglades" and/or the "Swamp Bandit." He was a known gangster who was involved in bank robberies. He robbed at least 40 banks totaling $1 million in heist profits. He also hindered the illegal whiskey trade by hijacking smuggled goods. By the time Ashley died, he was considered a folk hero due to his resistance towards bankers, landlords, and lawmen.

Al Capone also allegedly utilized the Lost City (a three-acre site full of rotted shacks and old artifacts area) for his illegal operations of making moonshine.

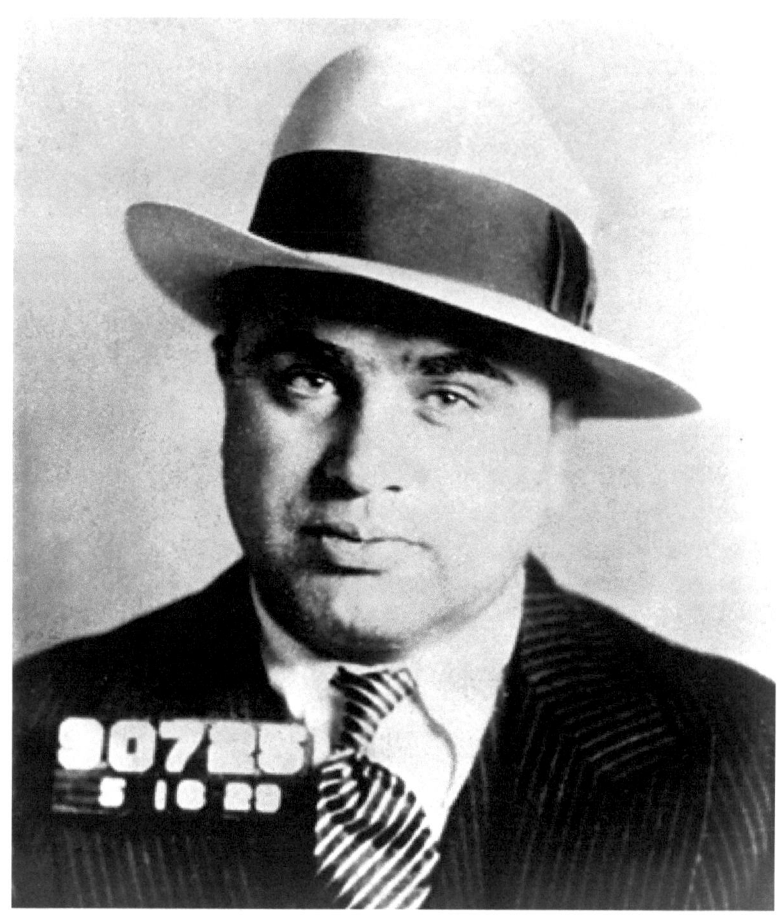

Mug Shot of Al Capone/ Photographic File of the Paris Bureau of the New York Times, The U.S. National Archives

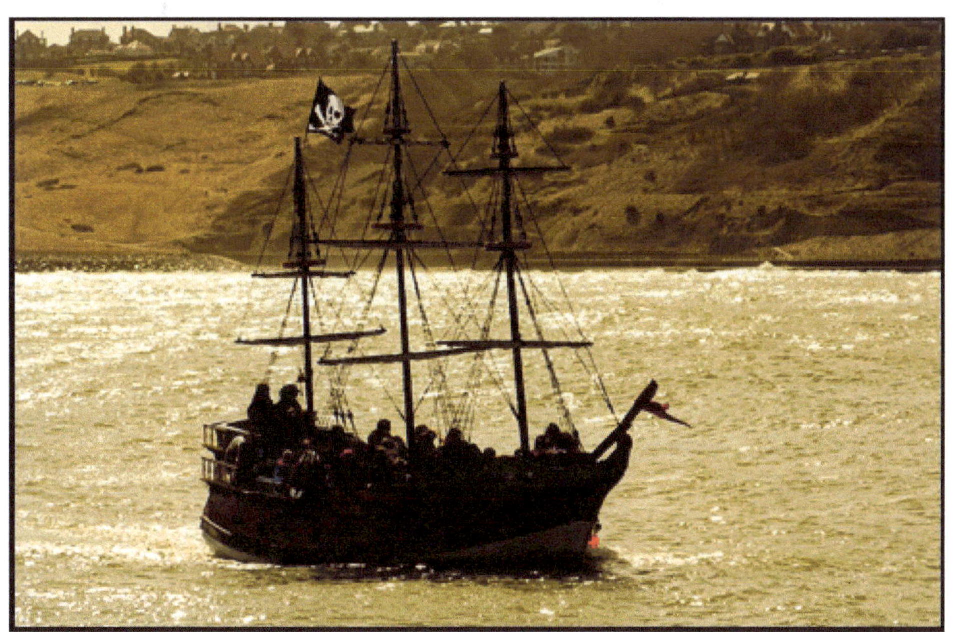

Ahoy, Pirates…!!!
Photo: George Hodan Public Domain Pictures / Public Domain

More than one body has been found belly up, floating on top of its waters.

Did you know there are even stories of cursed pirates that are seen sailing the Everglades as eternal punishment? Old tales tell us that after the pirates gave chase to a merchant ship for hours, angry by the chase the captain of the ship made all the crew members walk the plank. In addition, he also made the wife watch. It is said that she cursed them for eternity.

There are many more intriguing stories that highlight this wonderland's Good, Bad, and Ugly. Remote and isolated, the Everglades was, and is, the perfect hideout for shifty characters as they have been able to conceal their criminal mischief throughout time.

All these stories, tales, and legends do nothing to detract from this vast land's wild and exotic beauty. The tales of pilfering and horror just add to the mystique, as they can be fascinating and shocking for those family members that love history and excitement.

A great bird watching destination for bird lovers.

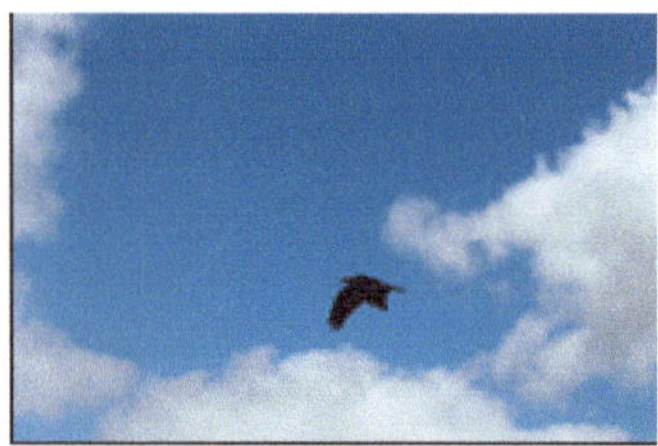

CPT Neal pointed out the different birds we came across in our journey. He gifted us with stories about those beautiful creatures that call the Everglades their home.

Over three hundred and fifty bird species fly in the vast skies above the Everglades.

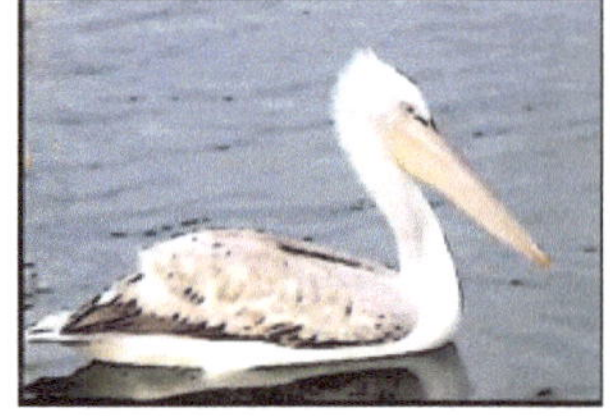

Some of them are wading birds such as the Purple Gallinule, nesting Bald Eagles, wintering wildfowl, migrating Hawks, Red Cockaded Woodpeckers, and Roseate Spoonbills. The Cormorants, Nesting Anhinga's, and many more are seen along the shores anytime of the day.

While there may be too many bird species to individually mention here, we have to give credit to the current Florida State bird, the Northern Mockingbird. Florida adopted this bird as their National symbol in 1927, however, a few other US states like Arkansas, Tennessee, Texas, and Mississippi

share the same state bird too. It is distinguishable by its grey and white feathers and most popular for its ability to sing songs, mimic people, and also mimic sounds from other animals.

As of October 2021 there have been 3 bills introduced into legislation in an attempt to change the state bird. The birds currently in the running are the Florida Scrub Jay, Flamingo, Osprey and Roseate Spoonbill. All 4 of these birds are native to Florida and can be found in the

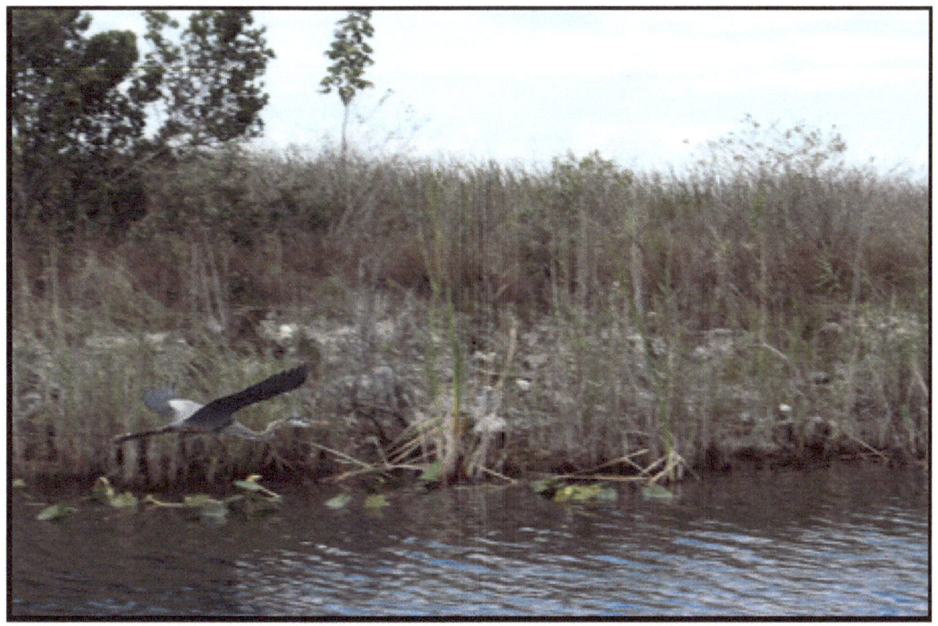

Everglades National Park.
I Fly/ Photo: Niurka Castaneda

The Everglades should be protected at all costs!!!

Plants Found in the Everglades

We saw many different types of plants and flowers during our adventure. Here are a few that we focused on and discussed in more detail.

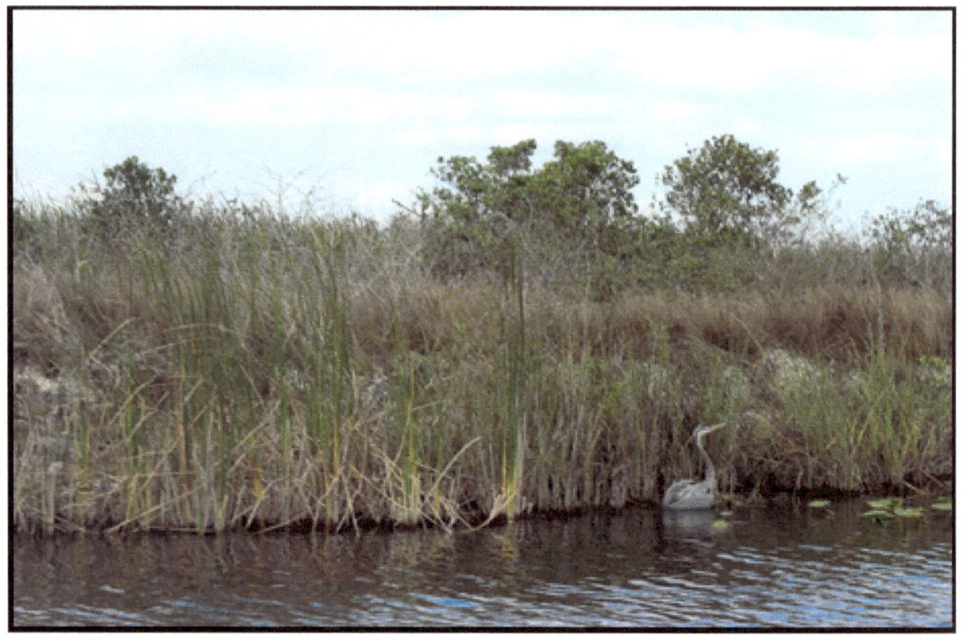

Photo: Niurka Castaneda

The most dominant plant throughout the Everglades is Sawgrass (also known as swamp grass). It is easily spotted throughout since it grows tall and lines most of the waters edge. Upon closer inspection, one can see tiny ridge like teeth lining the sawgrass. If one is not careful, this plant can cause small cuts that resemble paper cuts.

Another common plant we paid close attention to was the White Water Lily.

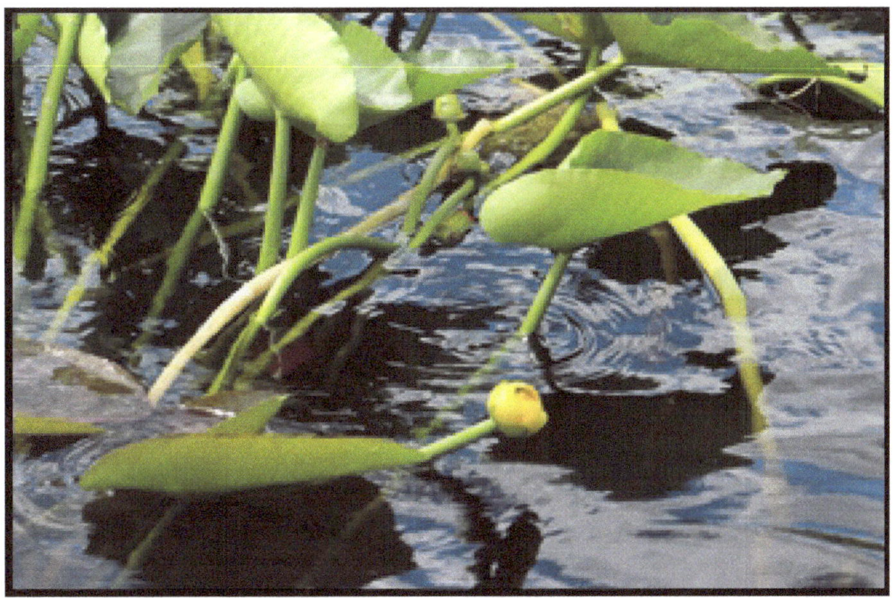

This is a beautiful fragrant flowering plan found in the waters as its name implies. The flower's petals open in the morning and close into the evening. While fishing, we would often cast our reels close to the White Lilly clusters being careful not to get tangled in their vast root systems beneath the lily pads' surface.

Captain Neal shared that fish can often be caught (and released) around these clusters.

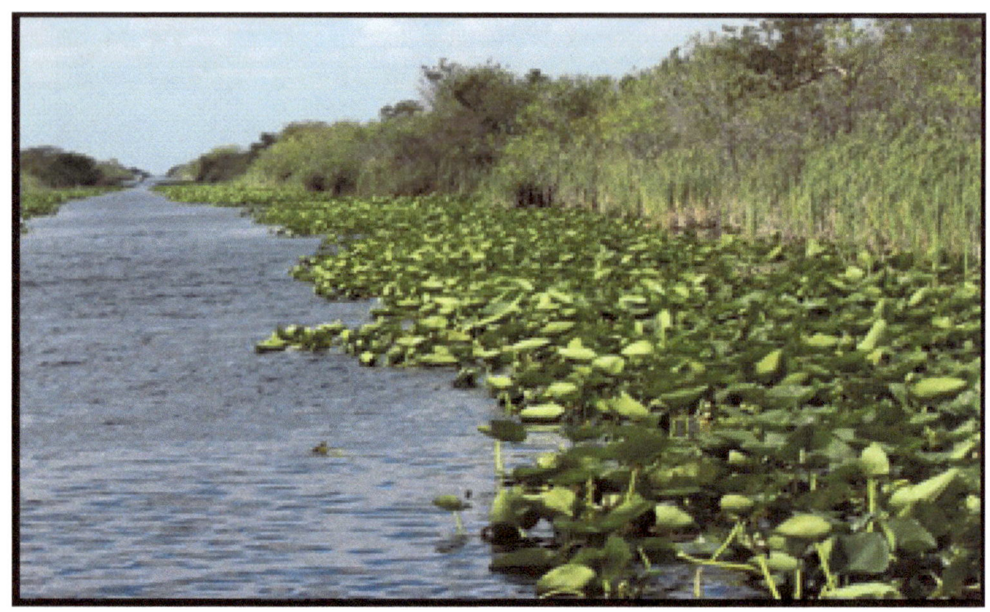

Did you know you can find apples in the Everglades? We did not!

CPT Neal surprised us by pointing out the Alligator Apples (Annona glabra), also known as the swamp apple, pond apple or monkey apple. It grows wild on the trees lining the water and is native to this area. It is a little tree with green leaves, the flower petals are white or a pale yellow color and very thick. The tree also bear a large fruit that tolerates salt water but cannot grow in dry soil.

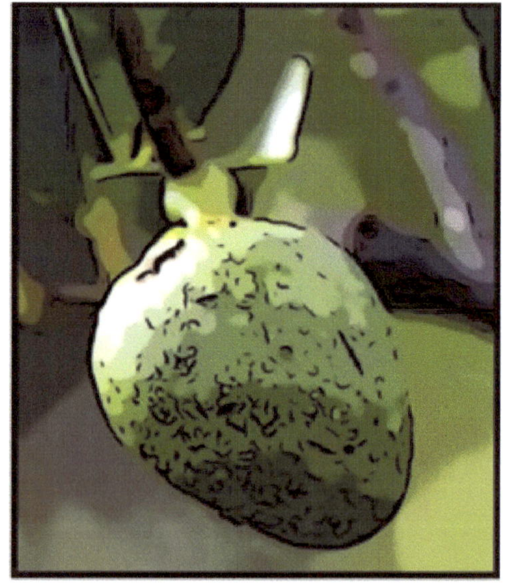

Photo: Niurka Castaneda

He explained that it was an edible apple…making me wonder if it would be possible to grab enough to make an organic apple pie.

However, he later explained that while the Natives, earlier settlers and many animals like the birds, raccoons, alligators and others were known to eat the fruit when ripe (yellow to red color during the fall and winter month), experts now advise against consuming it due to the seeds inside possibly being poisonous (100 seeds per fruit.) The toxic powder dust from the seeds have become notorious for blinding people. Recent studies have shown that the seeds have anticancer compounds. Some people said that they have dared to eat this fruit but it tastes a bit bland with just a hint of passion fruit.

IMPORTANT: This tree should not be confused with the Manchineel tree, which can also found in the South Florida Everglades. These "apples" are often referred to as the "Little Apple of Death." While looking seemingly harmless on the surface, it is important to know that the bark sap and fruit of the Manchineel tree can be detrimental to humans. Coming in contact can cause a wide range of rashes, inflammation, blindness or even prove fatal. In 2011 the Guinness Book of World Records identified the Manchineel tree as "the most dangerous tree in the world." Upon further research it is interesting to note that the natives used to line their arrows with the tree sap for battle purposes. While we love us some good old homemade American apple pie, this is one "apple" that I would respectfully suggest you avoid!

ANIMALS in the Everglades
Is it an alligator or a Crocodile?

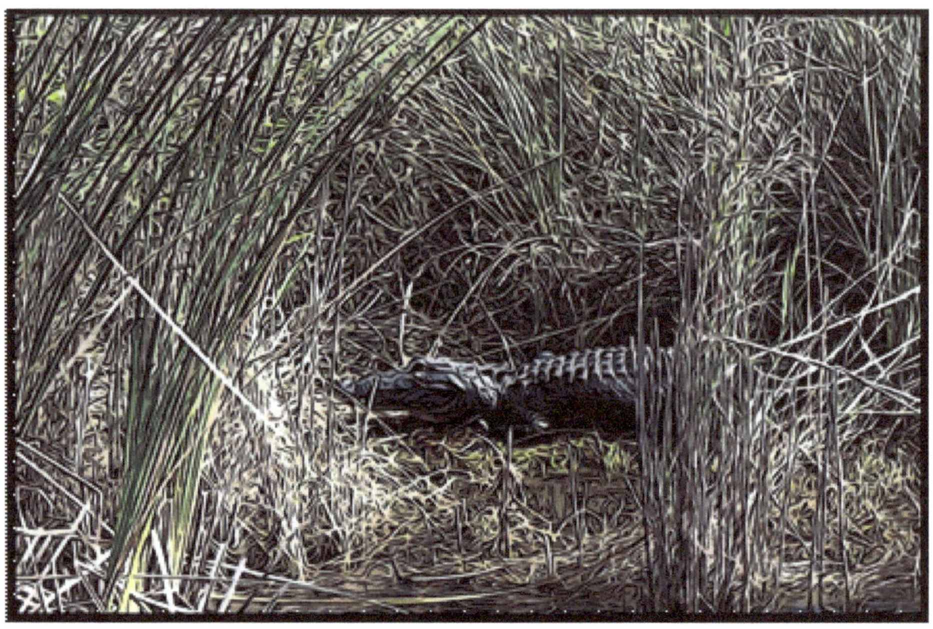

I see you, Alligator /Photo: Niurka Castaneda

Both the gators and the crocs call The Everglade's their home. You can differentiate the crocodiles from the alligators by their V-shaped snouts. Crocs seem like they are grinning at you while they keep their snouts closed, and the gators have more of a U-shaped serious look. Alligators are only found in the United States and certain parts of China...whereas crocs are found across the world.

Crocs are much larger, growing up to 20 ft at times, while alligators are smaller and reach a maximum of 15 ft in length. Alligators are not as aggressive as crocodiles and gators outnumber crocs greatly. While the Crocodile hangs in the pockets of saltwater, the Alligator prefers to hide in freshwater swimming alongside the sea turtle.

You can take an airboat ride to get close enough to touch crocs and gators, a favorite activity of many tourists…the airboat ride, NOT touching the gators/crocs part (for clarification purposes.)

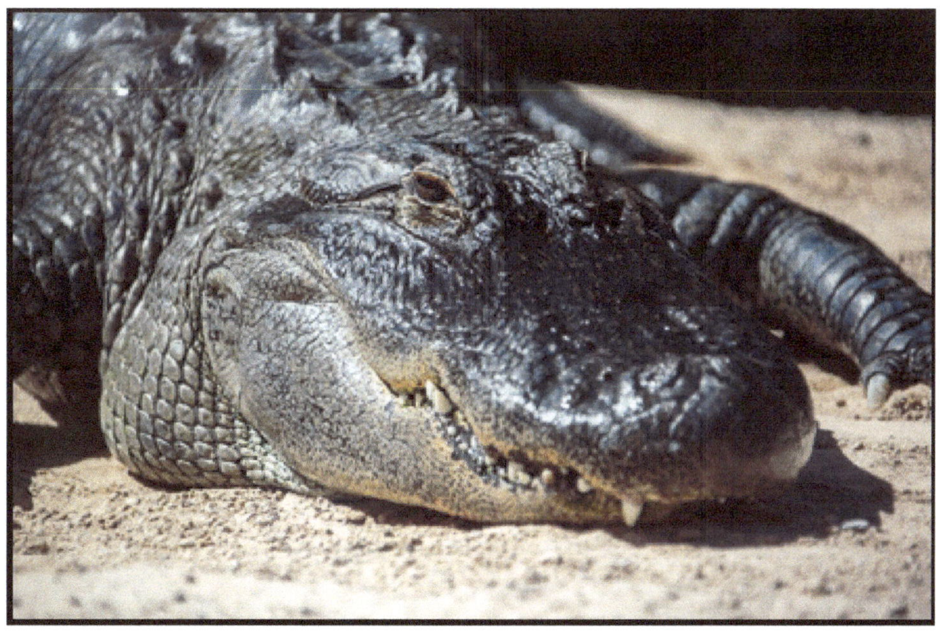

Crocodile resting/ Petr Kratochvil /Photo: CCO Public Domain

WARNING: DO NOT try to touch these "warm friendly" creatures.

Hunting snakes in the Everglades...

Hunting is also an organized activity that some can choose to participate in at the Everglades National Park (especially Veterans....insert sarcastic smiley emoji); The Python Elimination Program started in March 2017 and encourages a limited number of individuals to humanely eliminate and remove these destructive snakes which have become an invasive apex predator in the Everglades.

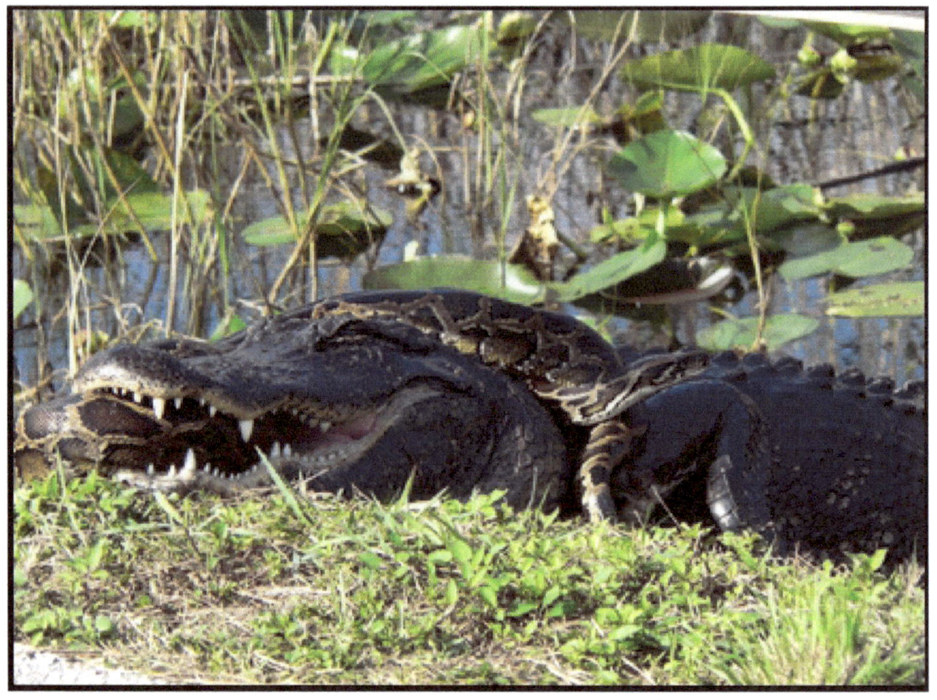

Alligator Eating a Python / Photo: Jean Beaufort / Public Domain Pictures / Public Domain

Without any natural predators to abate their growth has exploded with devastating consequences for other current residents population-like the rabbits, foxes, opossums, raccoons, etc that they like to feed on. The latest sighting has beed reported to be reduce to less than a 90% according to a study by NPS.

According to the South Florida Waste Management District (SFWMD) the person or individuals that choose to participate in this exhilarating program would get compensated.

There is a set $10 to $15 dollar hourly wage depending of the size of the area that is covered with a maximum of 10 hours at day. An additional $75 to $150 dollars can be earned for each 5" - 8" snake that is captured. Another $200 dollars can be earned once you are able to verify an active nest of hatchlings has been found.

In addition there is a 10 day annual competition that you can choose to participate in and that is called the Florida Python Challenge® . There is a prize of $10,000 dollars. It is hosted by the Florida Fish and Wildlife Conservation Commission (FWC), SFWMD, & Wildlife Foundation of Florida and the Fish (WFF), as part of a coordinated Everglades conservation effort.

BE WARNED: A Burmese python can grow to be 19" feet long... Be careful when practicing this sport! Wait, did you hear purring...?

That purring that you might be hearing comes from a beautiful wild cat with tan colored skin and piercing blue-green eyes...that may be silently stalking you through the bushes.

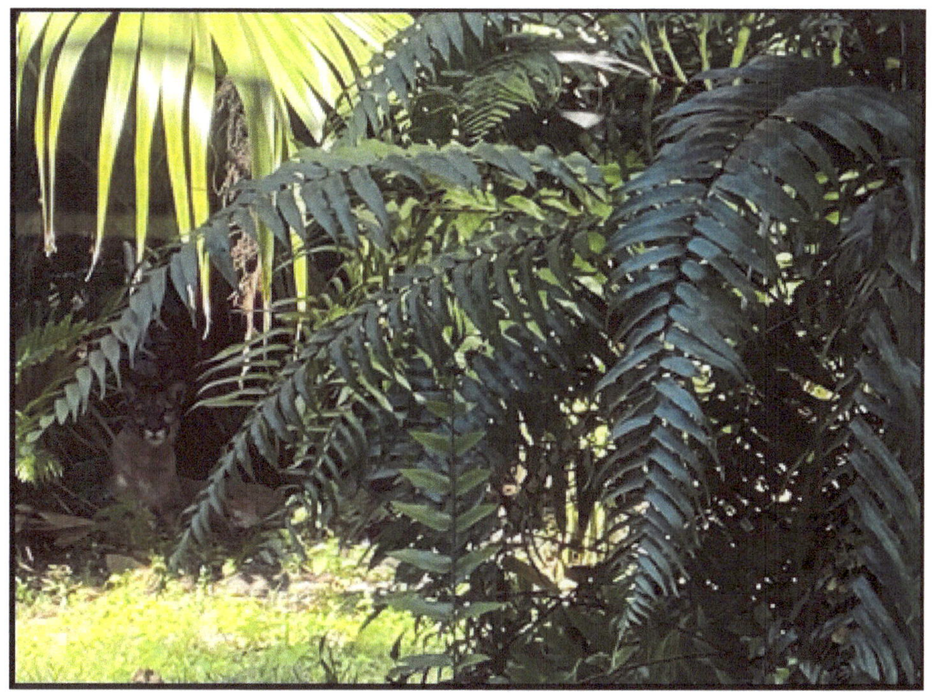

Stalking You / Photo: Niurka Castaneda

What is it? A jaguar, a cougar or a FL panther?

If you listen intently, you might hear them communicate by their unique Chirping, Hissing, Purring and Whistling sounds as they hunt. It is a Florida panther, one of the feline species that does not roar.

Many people mistake them for a jaguar.... when in fact it is in the Cougar family. The Fl panther is a subspecies of the cougar aka mountain lion / Puma family. It has been designated endangered species since 1967.

Be warned, they are wild predatory animals.

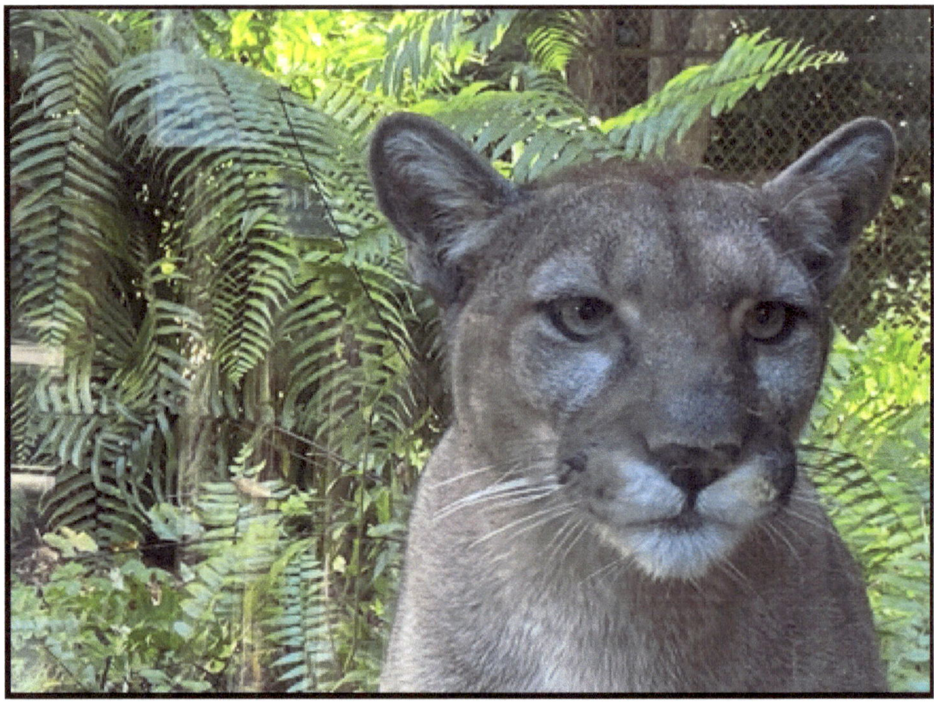

The Florida Panther / Photo: Niurka Castaneda

PLEASE DO NOT TRY TO TOUCH THE PANTHERS EITHER...safety first!

The perfect getaway for ALL!

If you are looking for a relaxing or adventurous outing, this is the place for you! Whether you are with friends or family, you can escape your routine daily life for something different. There is a little bit of everything that is sure to add to an unforgettable time.

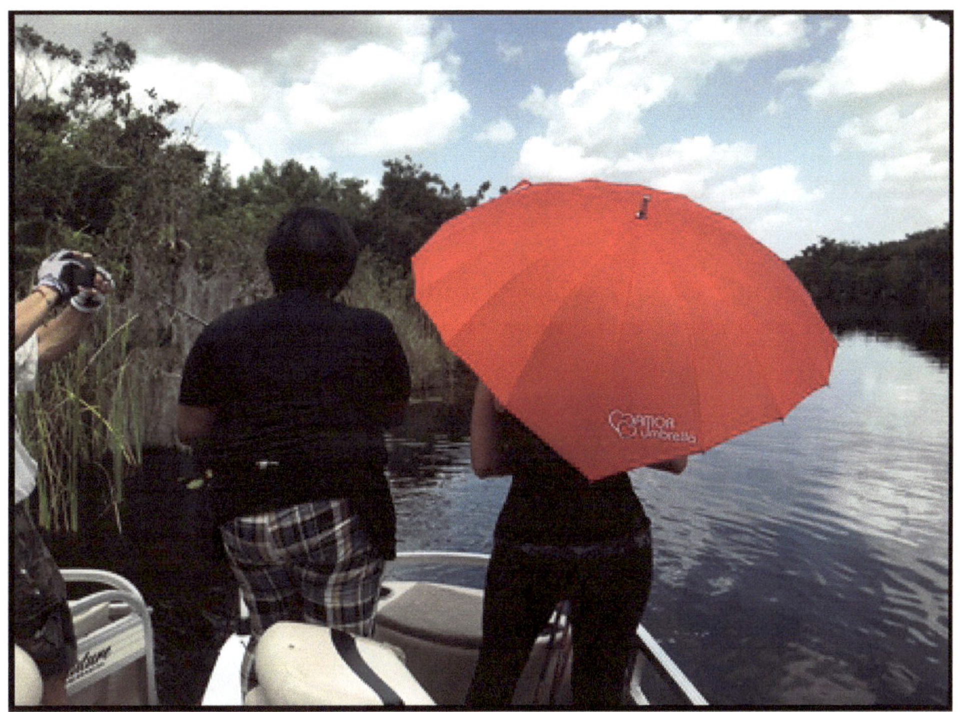

Photo: Niurka Castaneda

This alluring wild habitat attracts nature aficionados, bird watchers, and wilderness photographers that enjoy getting close and being present with their natural surroundings.

Anglers are attracted by the diverse and plentiful fishing opportunities lurking beneath the seemingly tranquil water.

Those that love history and excitement would be fascinated by discovering all the gory stories of pilfering and horror.

For us, it was an experience and opportunity to pause the day. Also allowing us to celebrate and capture small precious moments....which was HUGE!!!

Personally, it was a real revelation of the wonderful treasures that the Everglades have to offer. I was actually able to relax-escape for a little while…

Learning firsthand about the inner workings of the Everglades manmade and natural systems, was not only educational, but it was also fascinating.

This was not my first visit to the Everglades… but it was the first time I was able to take in the subtle beauty of the resilient and majestic "Pa-hay-Okee." Despite the years of withstanding the pure destructive force of tropical storms, fires, and flooding, it has not lost its strength and beauty.

I can clearly understand how this magical place was (and is) the source of inspiration for writers, poets, photographers, painters, and urban legends alike.

I can honestly tell you that I didn't want that day to end. Truth be told, it really hasn't. That journey to the Everglades has stayed present in my memories and daydreams since.

I enjoyed the warm sun on my face and the soft wind that flowed through my hair. I was able to relax and let go of the stressors in my life for at least a little while.

I had my camera. I had my friends…

I had my red "AMOR" umbrella to shield me from the sun.

And I now have a memory that will stay in my heart forever….

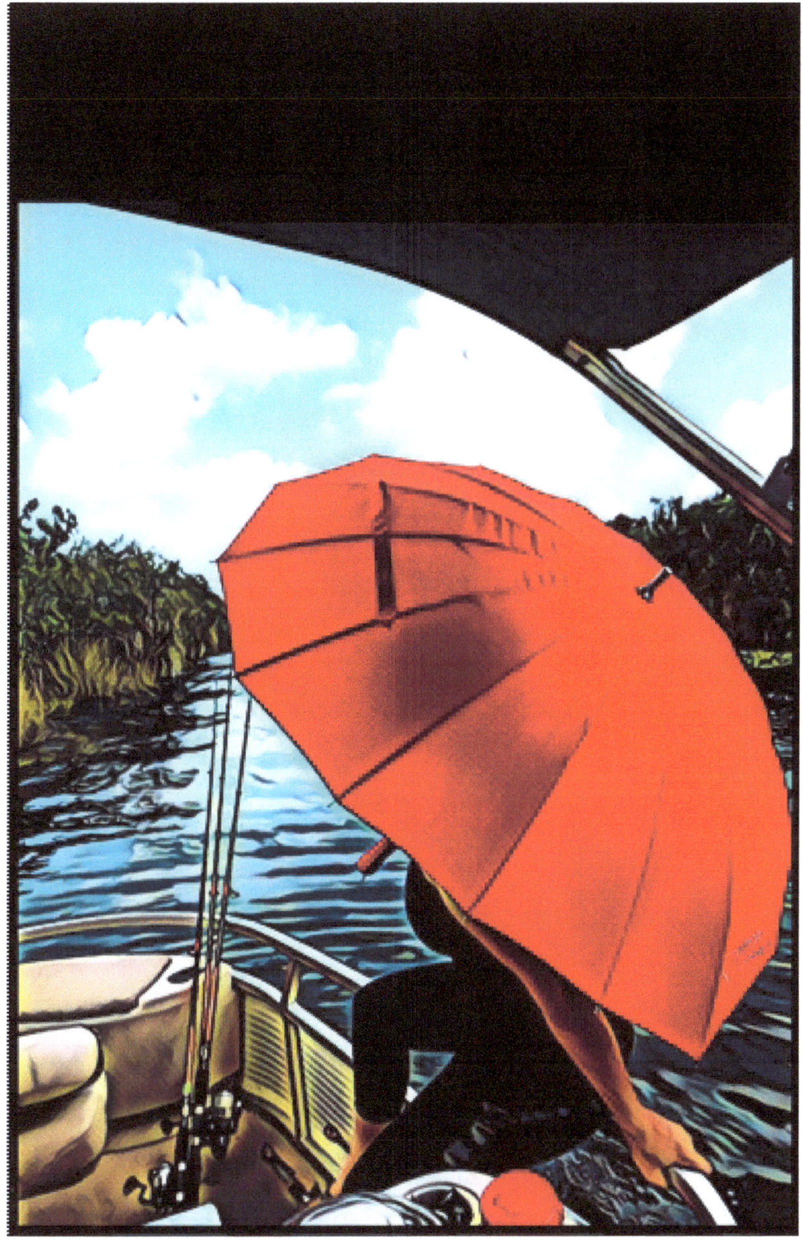

My red AMOR umbrella / Photo: Niurka Castaneda

Works Cited

(n.d.). Retrieved from http://www.news-press.com/apps/pbcs.dll/article?AID=2008803090405 (site inactive on 4 February 2022)

About the everglades: Captain Mitch's: Everglades Airboat Rides. Captain Mitch's * Everglades Airboat rides. (n.d.). Retrieved January 13, 2022, from http://www.captainmitchs.com/everglades

A Florida Crocodile. (n.d.). photograph. Retrieved from http://www.floridamemory.com/items/show/333031.

Bancroft, J. (2016, July 18). Creepy stories and legends about the Florida Everglades. Ranker. Retrieved January 13, 2022, from https://www.ranker.com/list/creepy-everglades-stories/jacobybancroft

Beaufort , J. (n.d.). Alligator And Python. photograph. Retrieved from https://www.publicdomainpictures.net/en/free-download.php?image=alligator-and-python&id=223232.

The benefits of photography on mental health, perspective and life. PhotoJeepers. (2021, January 14). Retrieved February 4, 2022, from https://photojeepers.com/benefits-of-photography-mental-health/

Castaneda, N. (n.d.). Everglades Flowing Waters. photograph.

Castaneda, N. (n.d.). I Fly. photograph.

Castaneda, N. (n.d.). I got caught. photograph.

Castaneda, N. (n.d.). I See You, Alligator. photograph.

Castaneda, N. (n.d.). My red AMOR umbrella. photograph.

Castaneda, N. (n.d.). Mother Nature's gauze . photograph.

Castaneda, N. (n.d.). National Everglades Park. photograph.

Castaneda, N. (n.d.). Of the Hook. photograph.

Castaneda, N. (n.d.). The Florida Panther. photograph.

Castaneda, N. (n.d.). The Stalking Florida Panther. photograph.

Castaneda, N. (n.d.). We dare. photograph.

Curti, M. (2021, May 11). Ornitherapy: The therapeutic power of birdwatching. BirdWatching. Retrieved February 4, 2022, from https://www.birdwatchingdaily.com/news/birdwatching/ornitherapy-therapeutic-power-birdwatching/

Dutton, N. (2013, January 10). PETA has warning for Burmese python hunters in Florida. WTVR. Retrieved February 4, 2022, from https://www.wtvr.com/2013/01/10/peta-has-warning-for-burmese-python-hunters-in-florida

Everglades' Deadly Manchineel Tree: Don't hug this one. American Council on Science and Health. (2020, February 27). Retrieved January 13, 2022, from https://www.test2.acsh.org/news/2020/02/16/everglades-one-bad-apple-does-spoil-whole-bunch-14574

Florida Python Challenge® Kicks of today; with new $10,000 award. Florida Fish And Wildlife Conservation Commission. (n.d.). Retrieved February 4, 2022, from https://myfwc.com/news/all-news/python-challenge-721/

Hodan, G. (n.d.). Pirate Ship At Sea. photograph. Retrieved from https://www.publicdomainpictures.net/en/view-image.php?image=37086&picture=pirate-ship-at-sea.

Kaye, K., & Sentinel, S. (2018, December 24). Solving mystery of 'lost city' in Everglades. sun. Retrieved January 13, 2022, from https://www.sun-sentinel.com/local/broward/fl-lost-city-20140517-story.html

Kratochvil, P. (n.d.). Crocodile. photograph. Retrieved from https://www.publicdomainpictures.net/en/view-image.php?image=249129&picture=crocodile.

'Little Apple of Death': Tree Found in South Florida Named World's Deadliest. 'little apple of death': Tree found in South Florida named World's deadliest. (n.d.). Retrieved January 13, 2022, from https://www.msn.com/en-us/news/us/little-apple-of-death-tree-found-in-south-florida-named-world-s-deadliest/ar-AAQPwRj

Miami Police Department, Public domain, via Wikimedia Commons. (n.d.). Al Capone in Florida. photograph. Retrieved from https://upload.wikimedia.org/wikipedia/commons/8/8c/Al_Capone_in_Florida.jpg.

Mighty Calusa. Barriers Island Park Society. (n.d.). Retrieved from https://www.barriersislandparksociety.org/mighty-calusa

Mowatt, R. A. (n.d.). (PDF) war narratives: Veteran stories, PTSD effects, and ... Retrieved February 4, 2022, from https://www.researchgate.net/publication/285800529_War_Narratives_Veteran_Stories_PTSD_Effects_and_Therapeutic_Fly-Fishing

Mug Shot of Al Capone. (n.d.). photograph. Retrieved from https://catalog.archives.gov/id/24520406.

Parks, A. O. (2021, July 6). Health benefits of fishing. Parks Blog. Retrieved February 4, 2022, from https://www.ontarioparks.com/parksblog/health-benefits-fishing/

Plants. Everglades National Park. (n.d.). Retrieved January 13, 2022, from https://everglades-nps-project.weebly.com/plants.html

Plant profile: Pond apple. Captain Mitch's * Everglades Airboat rides. (2016, July 18). Retrieved February 4, 2022, from http://www.captainmitchs.com/plant-profile-pond-apple/

Pennsylvania Department of Corrections / FBI, Public domain, via Wikimedia Commons. (n.d.). photograph, https://upload.wikimedia.org/wikipedia/commons/a/a4/Al_Capone_in_1929.jpg.

Schuknecht, C. (2019, April 8). 17-foot python in Florida breaks record, Park officials say. NPR. Retrieved February 4, 2022, from https://www.npr.org/2019/04/08/710972766/17-foot-python-in-florida-breaks-record-park-officials-say

Stalking the Florida panther. Florida RV Trade Association. (2020, September 14). Retrieved January 13, 2022, from https://www.frvta.org/stalking-the-florida-panther/

U.S. Department of Health and Human Services. (n.d.). Office of dietary supplements - vitamin D. NIH Office of Dietary Supplements. Retrieved February 4, 2022, from https://ods.od.nih.gov/factsheets/VitaminD-HealthProfessional/

U.S. Department of the Interior. (n.d.). Catch and release fishing. National Parks Service. Retrieved January 13, 2022, from http://www.nps.gov/subjects/fishing/catch-and-release-fishing.htm

U.S. Department of the Interior. (n.d.). A beginning for the park. National Parks Service. Retrieved February 4, 2022, from https://home.nps.gov/ever/learn/kidsyouth/a-beginning-for-the-park.htm

Thu, S. by F. on. (n.d.). Python elimination program. South Florida Water Management District. Retrieved February 4, 2022, from https://www.sfwmd.gov/our-work/python-program

ABOUT THE AUTHORS

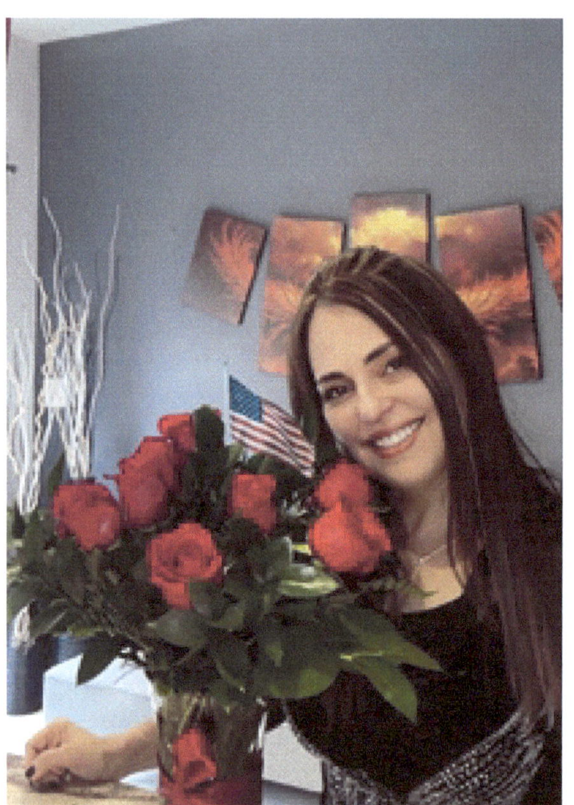

©Angelina Andreoni

The author, Masha Andreoni is the one that suggested and organized this trip. She is also helping me with this publication. As a licensed clinical social worker who is passionate about, dedicated to, and grateful for Veterans; she has chosen to dedicate much of her time/practice to serving those who have served and their families. She is also the founder of Empowered Veterans of America. Because of her strong beliefs in the therapeutic value of combing recreational therapy with traditional therapy... she coordinated this trip with her friend, Captain Neal Stark (Cpt.)

Learn more about her @ Empoweredveterans.com

ABOUT THE AUTHORS

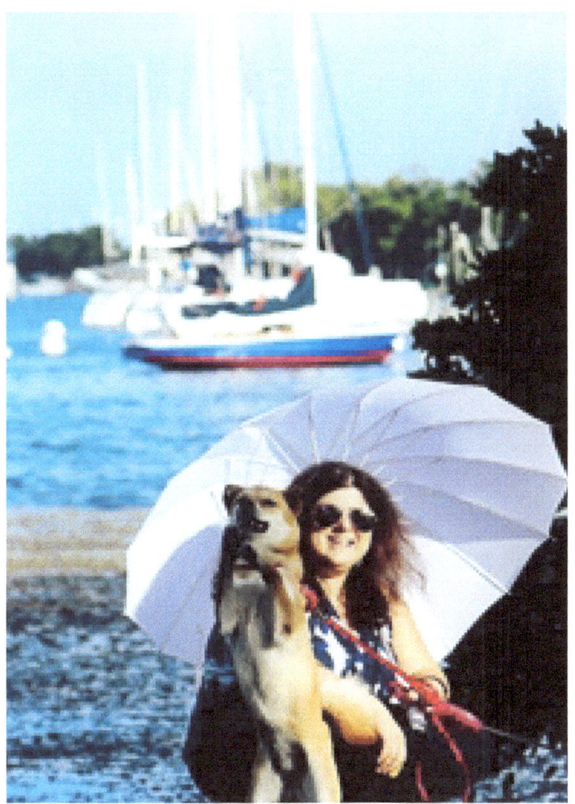

©Christine Sanchez

The author, Niurka Castaneda, is the mother of two incredible kids. She loves to write, travel, and take pictures. Entrepreneurship was a way to find her identity after transitioning from the military and building the brand Amor Umbrella out of a heart shaped, bright red umbrella. She is enthusiastic for veteran entrepreneurial journeys, and under the umbrella of Amor Umbrella Ventures, she focuses on education, media, and brand awareness to help inspire, ignite, and educate other veteran entrepreneurs in their own entrepreneurial journey.

Learn more about her @ NiurkaCastaneda.com

www.ingramcontent.com/pod-product-compliance
Lightning Source LLC
LaVergne TN
LVHW052300100826
845147LV00001B/100

* 9 7 8 1 7 3 6 4 8 1 5 0 9 *